It's About Time!
The Time Is Now

by

Phillip A. Ross

It's About Time!
The Time Is Now

ISBN: 978-0-9820385-0-5

Published by
Pilgrim Platform
149 E. Spring St., Marietta
Ohio, 45750
www.pilgrim-platform.org

Biblical quotations are from the *English Standard Version*, Standard Bible Society, unless otherwise cited.

The cover illustration suggests that the seasons of Advent and Lent are mutually dependent.

Printed in the United States of America

*For the Valley
of Dry Bones*

Goodnews—Evangel 2022, 187 pgs., 2023
Goodnews—Evangel 2023, 320 pgs., 2024
Goodnews—Evangel 2024, 300 pgs., 2025
The Heritage of St. Paul's Evangelical Church, 125 pgs., 2024

Books by Phillip A. Ross

The Work At Zion—A Reckoning, Two-volume set, 772 pgs., 1996.

Practically Christian—Applying James Today, 135 pgs., 2006.

The Wisdom of Jesus Christ in the Book of Proverbs, 414 pgs., 2006.

Marking God's Word—Understanding Jesus, 324 pgs., 2006.

Acts of Faith—Kingdom Advancement, 326 pgs., 2007.

Informal Christianity—Refining Christ's Church, 136 pgs., 2007.

Engagement—Establishing Relationship in Christ, 104 pgs., 1996, 2008.

It's About Time! — The Time Is Now, 40 pgs.. 2008.

The Big Ten—A Study of the Ten Commandments, 105 pgs., 2001, 2008.

Arsy Varsy—Reclaiming The Gospel in First Corinthians, 406 pgs., 2008.

Varsy Arsy—Proclaiming The Gospel in Second Corinthians, 356 pgs., 2009.

Colossians—Christos Singularis, 278 pgs., 2010.

Rock Mountain Creed—The Sermon on the Mount, 310 pgs., 2011.

The True Mystery of the Mystical Presence, 355 pgs., 2011.

Peter's Vision of Christ's Purpose in First Peter, 340 pgs., 2011.

Peter's Vision of The End in Second Peter, 184 pgs., 2012.

The Religious History of Nineteenth Century Marietta, Thomas Jefferson Summers, 124 pgs., 1903, 2012 (editor).

Conflict of Ages—The Great Debate of the Moral Relations of God and Man, Edward Beecher, 489 pgs., 1853, 2012 (editor).

Concord Of Ages—The Individual And Organic Harmony Of God And Man, Edward Beecher, D. D., 524 pgs., 1860, 2013 (editor).

Ephesians—Recovering the Vision of a Sustainable Church in Christ, 417 pgs., 2013.

Galatians: Backstory/Christory, 315 pgs., 2015.

Poet Tree—Root, Branch & Sap, 72 pgs., 2013.

Inside Out Woman—Collected Poetry, Doris M. Ross, 195 pgs., 2014 (editor).

God's Great Plan for the World—The Biblical Story of Creation and Redemption, 305 pgs., 2019.

John's Miracles—Seeing Beyond Our Expectations, 210 pgs., 2019.

Essays on Church—Ordinary Christianity for the World, 385 pgs., 2020.

Thessalonians—Thorn, Thistle, and Throne, 160 pgs., 2021.

Institutes of The Christian Religion, Emanuel V. Gerhart, 9 volumes, 2023 (ed).

TABLE OF CONTENTS

Introduction..1

Knowing The Times...............................1

Persevering The Times............................7

Suffering The Times..............................14

Sanctifying The Times...........................22

Beholding The Times.............................30

Understanding The Times....................36

What in the world is Ross doing?........43

INTRODUCTION

I am a pensive person by nature, or rather I should say that I am what I am because of what God created me to be, as are you. It's funny how saying such a simple thing can be so controversial—not the pensive part, the created part. We are all what we are because we have been created by God, both as individuals and as the cultures in which we live.

That simple statement about being created by God begs the question whether God created us to be sinners, since we are all sinners according to the Bible. Oops, I did it again. Sin is such a controversial subject. Not everyone believes it. If you don't, you may as well stop reading here because you won't be able to hear anything else I say. End of story—your story, not mine. Actually, the story is not mine, it's God's. I'm just trying to tell part of it. And because it's not my story I won't be saying anything new. But I will be telling it from my perspective, as we are all called to do.

This booklet is about thinking about God, the gospel, and Jesus Christ. We all need to make more time to do that. It is for the Mid-Ohio River Valley, but it is also for every valley where people live. It comes to a valley perspective from a valley perspective. This booklet is not about a mountaintop experi-

1

ence nor is it from a mountaintop perspective. Rather, it is from the "street," down in the valley where people actually live. It is not sad or morose, but it is serious—and it's about sin, yours and mine. It is an invitation to think more deeply about the things that we deeply care about, the things we believe. It's about Jesus.

These essays were originally given in 1998 as a short sermon series during Advent. I'm sure you will agree that they are not the usual Advent presentation of well-worn platitudes and biblical pablum. Unlike too many of my peers, I can't stomach that kind of stuff. To me, warm milk not only tastes bad, but it makes me sleepy.

This booklet is about the time in which we live. Hopefully, you will find it to be timely in your own life, as well. Time is a funny thing. We all live in it. Most of us are slaves to it, driven by appointments and schedules that must be kept. Asking people to think about time is like asking a fish to think about water—with one important difference. As far as we know, fish can't think at all, at least not in the way that we define thinking. I will ask you to think about time, about how much time you have, how much you need, and what you do with it.

This booklet is about schedules and appointments—not ours, but God's. God is also on a schedule and has appointments to make, and a timetable to keep. He has appointments with you and with me. He'll eventually meet with everyone because He has some things to go over, some accounts to close. It'll be an important meeting, so I'm hoping to help you think about it, even though there isn't much you can do to prepare for it. But there is this one thing that you can do. It's probably not what you think it is, but it is important. And so I'm trying to help you think about it by thinking about it myself.

Think of it as a gift, a gift that you can't really refuse, a gift that goes on giving. But it's not a gift *for* you, it's a gift *through* you—maybe, hopefully. I suppose it depends on whether you "get it" or not.

Phillip A. Ross
April 2008
Marietta, Ohio

KNOWING THE TIMES

Besides this you know the time, that the hour has come for you to wake from sleep. For salvation is nearer to us now than when we first believed. The night is far gone; the day is at hand. So then let us cast off the works of darkness and put on the armor of light. Let us walk properly as in the daytime, not in orgies and drunkenness, not in sexual immorality and sensuality, not in quarreling and jealousy. But put on the Lord Jesus Christ, and make no provision for the flesh, to gratify its desires.   —Romans 13:11-14

What would you have done had you lived in Germany in 1943? The Second World War was raging. Hitler was in power. Germany had come out of a tremendous recession and hyperinflation, her factories were producing again. The economy was good, in fact it was great.

Hitler's forces had successfully infiltrated the German Protestant church and his ministers and biblical scholars were producing much supporting material for the God-given right of the German people to seek additional living space at the expense of what they considered to be less worthy peoples and nations. Some German pastors joined the Brownshirts and supported Hitler and his National Socialist Party. Hitler didn't steal any elections or worm his way into power. He was elected by popular vote. You know the story, but what would you have done had you lived there then?

What would you have done had you lived in America in 1928, just prior to the 1929 market crash? Maybe some of you did. What did you do? Because the Great Depression came during a time of relatively primitive communications (by today's standards), I suspect that most people were taken by surprise by the Great Depression. Suddenly the banks had no money. Nonetheless, I'm just as sure that there were a few prophets of doom on the scene, predicting and warning people of the impending crash. I wonder whether they were conservative or liberal? Christian or not? Would you have listened to them? Or would you have dismissed them as fanatics—extremists.

One more. Imagine that you lived in Jerusalem in the A.D. 50s. The crucifixion of Jesus would have occurred during your lifetime, assuming you were an adult. The church according to Acts would have been in full swing. The Roman government would have been hunting and persecuting believers.

What were the Apostles and disciples preaching? Salvation by the blood of Christ to be sure, but they were also preaching the immanent return of Christ in judgment. The message would have been that Christ had come to provide salvation for His people, but had been rejected and crucified only to be resurrected in glory. And they would have been preaching that He was due back any day to render judgment, condemning the unfaithful to the fires of hell and taking the faithful bodily into heaven.

Imagine yourself living during those times. What would you do? How would you respond? How would you prepare for Christ's return?

GET BACK

Enough of vain imaginations. Let's return to the present. You now live in a global village. Modern communications and travel technologies have made the entire world accessible. Jet planes can take us anywhere in a matter of a day or two, and the Internet and cell phones make international communication virtually instantaneous from anywhere to anywhere.

Yet, the past hundred years or so have been marred by the greatest proliferation of wars and military conflicts in the history of the world. More Christians have been martyred during the Twentieth Century than all previous centuries together. We are currently experiencing a period of increased natural disasters—fires, floods, earthquakes, tornadoes, hurricanes, mudslides, etc. The previously belligerent governments of just a couple decades ago are now working together in a variety of ways. Scientists have successfully cloned several species of animals. The future has arrived. You get the picture?

Imagine that today is the first Sunday of Advent, Christmas is coming. But what does that mean? Traditionally that means that we prepare ourselves for the celebration of Jesus' birth. During the month preceding Christmas, we prepare our hearts and minds for the coming of Christ. Culturally, we also prepare our space, our environment. Christmas is an American cultural event, regardless of one's belief in Christ.

Every effort is made in the world of consumer economics to do Christmas without Jesus. Apparently, Jesus is too sweet or not sweet enough, so people choose Santa, the saccharine Holiday substitute. We decorate our yards and houses—inside and out. Christmas music becomes ubiquitous, and we spend money like drunken sailors. The Christmas season is the greatest retail season of the year. Many retail companies do half or more of their yearly business during the month of December. Christmas is a major cultural event.

But Christmas in America is increasingly without Christ—which is weird.

Every Christian I know becomes schizophrenic during the month of December. We love to complain about the commercialization of Christmas; how the decorations start so early, how the congestion in the stores puts people on edge, causing many of them to react in rudeness rather than in the spirit of Christmas; how children are spoiled with so many needless luxuries, etc. I'm sure you all know the litany well. I'll listen to your complaints if you will listen to mine.

Yet, we all love the romantic reason for the Season—*presents*. Oops, I mean *giving*. We also love to decorate our homes. We love to shop, and to be generous to those we love—especially ourselves. We learned our self-esteem in school. We love the smell of pine and mulled cider. We love the chill in the air and the anticipation of families getting together. We love visiting and catching up on family news. We love the Christmas season.

Yet we hate it. We detest how material it has become; how awful and gaudy the decorations seem to be this year; how inane the insipid music sounds—it's either too much Jesus or not enough. And at the same time we love how romantic it is. We are ourselves conflicted.

TWILIGHT ZONE
Christmas marks the passing of time, it is a seasonal celebration. We lament how quickly Christmases come and go.

The distance between them grows shorter every year. As a seasonal marker Christmas takes on a characteristic that separates it from the normal humdrum passage of time. Christmas is a special time, a unique time, an uncommon time of the year. It is a time in which ordinary concerns are set aside, as much as possible, a time in which the extraordinary graces of God are brought to the fore. It is a time in which many normal activities are suspended. It is a time of special events.

We encourage each other to forget the mundane and petty concerns of our normal lives and focus on the deeper, eternal things, Holiday and Seasonal things. But in doing so we enter into a kind of spiritual twilight zone, in which we encourage one another to focus on a romanticized, ideal world where everything is okay and no one ever grows up. We all pretend to believe in Santa and Jesus and other figments of Christmas. We smile and nod, meet and greet—and eat.

Awakening

Paul wrote to the Romans in the late A.D. 50's, bidding them to love one another, "you know the time, that the hour has come for you to wake from sleep. For salvation is nearer to us now than when we first believed" (v. 11). Salvation, while it is realized in an instant, takes a lifetime to assimilate. Our salvation does not whisk us out of this perishing world, at least not right away. Rather, salvation equips us for a lifetime of service in this world. Christ does not call His people out of this world, but into the world to be ambassadors of His salvation. Christianity is not an escapist, other-worldly religion, but a confrontive, this-world religion.

Consequently, Christianity requires two perspectives to operate simultaneously—the "already" and the "not yet." Christians must be aware of the unfolding of the great historical epochs, and of the specific period in which they live. A human lifetime comprises only a sliver of time compared to the biblical story.

Two Views, Three Periods

The time frame considered in the Bible is immense. It is a story that unfolds over thousands of years, and it unfolds in the reality of human history. There are three basic time periods that are the subject of Scripture: the Old Testament period that established the foundations, the New Testament period of the extension and expansion of God's kingdom (also called the Church), and the final period that will be characterized by the fulfillment of God's kingdom on earth, the time that is alluded to in the Book of Revelation, the time inaugurated by Jesus' second coming and is still anticipated today.

Christian time is measured by two points on a continuum. Christ's birth marks one end, and Christ's return marks the other. The time between these two historic and epochal events is known by various names. *Kairos* is a Greek word that means special or extraordinary time. Paul used *kairos* when he wrote to Timothy that "in later times (*kairos*) some will depart from the faith by devoting themselves to deceitful spirits and teachings of demons" (1 Timothy 4:1). Paul had in mind the *kairos* time between Christ's birth and His return, especially those times closer to Christ's return, which Paul eagerly anticipated.

That time, *kairos* time, is now. It has begun and it is not yet over. *We* live in the midst of it. God is still writing His story in our time. We are now closer to the end point or culmination of God's story than any other Christians in history. There has never been a time like this.

Are you ready? How will you get ready? What can you do? What will you do?

PERSEVERING THE TIMES

For whatever was written in former days was written for our instruction, that through endurance and through the encouragement of the Scriptures we might have hope. May the God of endurance and encouragement grant you to live in such harmony with one another, in accord with Christ Jesus, that together you may with one voice glorify the God and Father of our Lord Jesus Christ. —Romans 15:4-6

P aul counseled the Christians to redeem the time because "the days are evil" (Ephesians 5:16). And just as the Old Testament applied to the Christians in New Testament times, so both testaments continue to apply today. Scripture was written for our benefit and learning, and the days in which we live are still evil. They are, however, not merely evil.

The wheat and the tares are growing together. And an untended garden tends to get weedy.

It doesn't take a genius to see just how evil the times are, unfortunately it is everywhere evident. But because of the nature of the world in which we live we, as Christians, must manifest patience in all that we do and say. We must be patient with others because God is patient with us. Patience is a fruit of the Spirit. People are patient as a result of God's presence in their lives, and for no other reason. While other people can act patiently, no one can genuinely be patient unless they are led by God's Holy Spirit.

This simple understanding provides a great lesson for and about those who cannot control their tempers. Indeed, only God can control our temper, so where it is not controlled, God's Spirit is not manifest. We all struggle from time to time with our temper. But a lack of increasing control and/or growth in this regard can only indicate a lack of the presence of the Holy Spirit and of His salvation, where salvation is understood to include, not merely justification by God in heaven, but one's sanctification or growth in holiness on earth. Salvation always includes both justification and sanctification, both God's mercy and our growth in holiness. So, some lack of growth is certainly tolerable, even ordinary. But a consistent failure to grow over long periods of time suggests a lack of the Spirit.

HEARING

Paul said that the Bible was written for our benefit, which means that we must be involved in learning Scripture. Again, we come to the study of the Scriptures as the foundation of a genuine Christian life. Faithfulness means learning—not only learning, of course, but it always includes learning. Learning is not a requirement of faithfulness, but it is a fruit of faithfulness. And where study and learning are not practiced there is no faithfulness. And where there is no faithfulness there is no salvation.

Thus, it is essential that every Christian—and particularly those involved in church leadership—be engaged in Bible study because as Christians, and even more as leaders, we are called to manifest an extra measure of faithfulness. That's what leadership is about! Furthermore, church leaders should be involved in Bible study in the life of the church in which they are leaders, with the people that they are called to lead—and not just once in a while but regularly. In this way they demonstrate their faithfulness among those they lead. Evangelists will study with people outside the church as a way to reach the lost, but church leaders need to engage the people—church members—they are leading.

The word *patience* can also be translated as *perseverance*. The King James Version translated it as *longsuffering*. It suggests steadfastness, constancy, and endurance—the characteristic of a person who is not distracted from the deliberate purpose and loyalty to his faith and piety, not even by trials or sufferings. A patient person is one who attends to his duty even when he doesn't feel like it.

Scripture doesn't use *patience* to mean passively waiting around for something to happen. Rather, it uses it in the active sense of "hanging in there," keeping up the good fight, remaining committed under duress and difficulty. Knowing that it is darkest just before the dawn provides hope through the blight of the night in the midst of the fight, the fight to be patient and to persevere in faithfulness.

Sometimes we get frustrated with God's patience. Sometimes it seems like God ought not be so patient because His patience seems to allow so much evil in the world. We sometimes think that His patience is the cause of the evil and troubles of this world. Why doesn't God do anything about it? However, we need to be careful with the suggestion that God ought not be so patient. If God were any less patient, He might be less patient with *us*, with *you* and *me*. And we usually need His extra patience. I do, don't you?

The point is that the Spirit of God in relationship with a human being issues forth in patience and knowledge, or study and perseverance. Another way to say it is that God's Holy Spirit provides the patience of discipline that we need in order to persevere in our Bible study and grow in godliness.

HOPE

Everybody in this perishing world needs hope and encouragement. But where do hope and encouragement come from? Paul said Christians derive hope "through endurance and through the encouragement of the Scriptures" (v. 4). The source of our hope and comfort is the Bible. Christians receive hope by reading and studying the Bible. God provides it, and He provides it through study of the Scriptures. He doesn't just zap people... well, in a way He does. But God's zapping always produces fruit. So, if there isn't any fruit, you may be kidding yourself about having been zapped.

The practical application of this is that when we are not experiencing sufficient hope and comfort from our faith, we need to increase our Bible study. So, if you aren't feeling sufficiently encouraged or spiritually fed, if you find yourself struggling with hope, you need to spend more time in your Bible. We can't expect anyone else to prop up our flagging zeal— including the preacher. Don't depend on the preacher to meet your spiritual needs. Don't depend on a weekly sermon to satisfy the spiritual desires of your soul. Depend on Christ alone. And where do we encounter Christ? Through Scripture —and preaching, of course. But an hour a week does not a relationship make.

God has promised to feed His people abundantly, and God makes no empty promises. So, if you are feeling spiritually hungry, it's not because there's nothing to eat. God's Word is full of the nourishment you need. If you are hungry, in all like-lihood you aren't eating what's on your plate.

Too many Christians lust after someone else's sanctifica-tion. They want to be like this or that famous Christian, but too often they aren't willing to put in the time themselves. Rather, they want God to just zap them into the next level of sanctification. If only there were a God pill. We could just take it and be done with the difficulties. But it doesn't work like that. The difficulties serve as a necessary catalyst for the comfort, which comes through the discipline of faithfulness.

LIKEMINDED

Paul prayed that God would grant Christians the blessing of like-mindedness—that is, in the likeness of Jesus Christ—in order that they may glorify God. God is glorified as Christians become more and more like Christ, not like one another—not even like other famous Christians. The unity of the faith is not a matter of all Christians being like one another, but a matter of all Christians being like Christ. Christian unity is not a matter of all Christians belonging to the same church, denom-ination or organization, it's a matter of all Christians belonging to Christ, a matter of all Christians striving to become like Christ, that Christians manifest Christ-likeness in their lives.

In this is the unity of the Spirit! Here is the glory of God! God's glory is not found in a grand religious corporation that includes all of the denominations. God's glory is not found in cookie-cutter Christians spouting platitudes designed to increase their self-esteem. God's glory is not found by believing the latest theologians, be they liberationists, feminist, neo-orthodox, restorationist, emergent—whatever. God's glory is found by believing in Christ, and Christ cannot be believed apart from knowing Scripture. Neither can knowing Scripture happen apart from belief in Christ. Belief in Christ and knowledge of Scripture are mutually dependent.

Sure, it can and must begin with a little knowledge. But if it remains at that level, it isn't really belief. It's stony ground Christianity (Matthew 13:5), where the seed finds a little nourishment in the cracks, but fails to sink roots deep enough to draw water in the heat of the afternoon sun. So, "when the sun rose they were scorched. And since they had no root, they withered away" (Matthew 13:6).

THESE DAYS

These days are bad—evil, but they are not as bad as they are going to get. Paul wrote to Timothy that "all who desire to live a godly life in Christ Jesus will be persecuted, while evil people and impostors will go on from bad to worse, deceiving and being deceived. But as for you, continue in what you have learned and have firmly believed, knowing from whom you learned it and how from childhood you have been acquainted with the sacred writings, which are able to make you wise for salvation through faith in Christ Jesus" (2 Timothy 3:12-15). Is this still true? Of course it is. Has the end come yet? No.

Our ability to persevere is not diminished by the evil of the times in which we live. No matter how bad things get Christians always have the ability in Christ to live godly lives by the power and presence of the Holy Spirit through regeneration. The ability to persevere is provided by Christ, as He is encountered and engaged though Scripture.

Jesus Christ has already conquered this evil world, we just need to realize it and seek refuge where the refuge actually is—

in Christ. Our perseverance in the faith does not depend upon our strength, but on Christ's. Christ is the strength of the faithful. Christ is our perseverance. Christ will provide for us all the long-suffering we need. Praise be to God!

SUFFERING THE TIMES

Be patient, therefore, brothers, until the coming of the Lord.
See how the farmer waits for the precious fruit of the earth,
being patient about it, until it receives the early and the late
rains. You also, be patient. Establish your hearts, for the
coming of the Lord is at hand. Do not grumble against one
another, brothers, so that you may not be judged; behold,
the Judge is standing at the door. As an example of
suffering and patience, brothers, take the prophets who
spoke in the name of the Lord. Behold, we consider those
blessed who remained steadfast. You have heard of the
steadfastness of Job, and you have seen the purpose of the
Lord, how the Lord is compassionate and merciful.
—*James 5:7-11*

The word *suffer* has several meanings. It means to experience something painful or unpleasant. It also means to experience something in the sense of to endure or bear something. And finally it also means to permit or allow something, as when Jesus said, "Suffer little children, and forbid them not, to come unto me" (Matthew 19:14—KJV). *Suffer* means to experience, to endure, to allow.

14

James counsels Christians to be patient as we wait for the coming of the Lord. We are to suffer these times, for they have been appointed to precede the coming of the Lord. The Lord will not come again until the fulfillment of these times in which we now live, and these times will not be fulfilled until all that has been prophesied has come to be.

These days of moral crisis in which we live may be a prelude to worse times. I suspect they are because Scripture tells us that sinners will grow worse over time (2 Timothy 3:12-15). My intent in discussing this issue is not to scare people, but to prepare Christians that they may suffer or endure the times. What times?

> *And as He sat on the Mount of Olives, the disciples came to Him privately, saying, Tell us, when shall these things be? And what shall be the sign of Your coming, and of the end of the world? And Jesus answered and said to them, Take heed that no man deceive you. For many will come in My name, saying, I am Christ, and will deceive many. And you will hear of wars and rumors of wars. See that you are not troubled, for all these things must occur; but the end is not yet. For nation will rise against nation, and kingdom against kingdom. And there will be famines and pestilences and earthquakes in different places. All these are the beginning of sorrows. Then they will deliver you up to be afflicted and will kill you. And you will be hated of all nations for My name's sake. And then many will be offended, and will betray one another, and will hate one another. And many false prophets will rise and deceive many. And because iniquity shall abound, the love of many will become cold. But he who endures to the end, the same shall be kept safe. (Matthew 24:3-13).*

While this discourse by Jesus was about the destruction of Jerusalem that came to pass in A.D. 70, it also serves as a type in that it suggests some principles or patterns regarding God's judgment, which according to the biblical testimony is a recurring historical theme. We are seeing a number of these kinds of patterns in the current era. However, we must neither rush to a conclusion, nor deny the evidence. Surely we are closer to the end of history than any previous generation, but every generation could say that. The Advent season provides an opportunity to consider the times in which we live, as we anticipate the coming again, not only of Christmas, but of Christ Himself.

TRIBULATION

It doesn't take a genius to see that we live in the midst of war and strife. It could be worse—a lot worse, no doubt. Nonetheless, we live during a time of tremendous warring among the nations. There are a growing number of famines, pestilences, and earthquakes in various places. In addition, over the past one hundred years have been an increasing number of reports of serious Christian persecution and tribulation among Christians in foreign countries.

If the United Nations continues in the direction it is going, it won't be long before several foundational Christian beliefs will be outlawed in many nations. Already in Canada it is illegal to read certain sections of Scripture on the public airwaves—those dealing with homosexuality. Think about that. It is against the law in Canada to read sections of the Bible on the radio or in a public place.

The issue under attack is the First Commandment, "You shall have no other gods before Me" (Exodus 20:3). God is not tolerant of other religions and their false gods, and forbids His people to indulge in such false beliefs and practices. We must see that the effort toward religious toleration is an attack upon the First Commandment, an effort to eliminate it from public awareness and use.

Now that doesn't mean that Christians are to be unkind toward others who believe differently. The First Commandment is not an excuse for war, genocide, or any other nastiness toward other people. Quite the opposite, Jesus calls us to love our enemies. We are to emulate God's mercy in the face of sin. But this does in fact mean that God's truth is objective, and faithful Christians are not free to interpret or disregard Scripture as they like.

Rather, God's truth must be received as it has been given. Scripture is to interpret Scripture. The point is that God does not tolerate His people to believe in falsehoods. He forbids us to believe anything untrue. He wants us to only believe what is true because all truth is His, and all truth gives God glory. The kind of religious toleration that is being promoted today mandates that Christians believe what the Bible teaches to be false.

OFFEND

This message about God's truth is destined to offend many people, just as Jesus said it would. "And then many will be offended, and will betray one another, and will hate one another" (Matthew 24:10). Those who oppose Christianity will twist this teaching and try to make it mean what Jesus doesn't say. They will interpret it to be nasty and vindictive when it is only a simple statement of the truth and adheres to the First Commandment as an engine of peace and prosperity.

Where there are many religions and those religions logically contradict one another, they cannot all be true. To say that you believe them all, or that they are all true, or that you are able to discern what is true in them and what is not, is pure nonsense. Religious discernment is beyond both reason and science. Neither can provide any insight into the truth or viability of religion. Such determinations belong to God alone and are provided in the Bible. Believing otherwise is forbidden by the First Commandment.

Nonetheless, we must be patient and kind toward those who believe falsely because at one time or another we have all believed falsely. We must understand that if people are not free to go to hell, salvation means nothing. No one is born a Christian, no one believes the gospel naturally. Hell is our natural destination. All Christians once believed falsely. All Christians once behaved in ways that displease God.

We cannot force people to believe rightly. We cannot force people to behave morally. We cannot force people out of their commitment to go to hell. Christians are not better than other people. We can only present the gospel and pray that the Holy Spirit will convert people from their wrong ideas and behaviors, for only the Holy Spirit can change hearts.

Yet, neither can we sit idly by while blatant sinners impose their immorality and hell-bent tendencies upon our neighbors and children. Friendship means caring for our friends. We are obligated as parents to protect our children from harm and teach them things that will benefit them. But what can we do when we live in the midst of a culture gone mad, a culture in love with sin?

Presenting the gospel is not only the only thing we can do, but it is the only thing that offers any genuine hope because only the power of the gospel can genuinely convert people to Christ. We must begin by presenting the gospel to our own children and grandchildren. I don't simply mean getting them to pray some prayer, but rather, we must demonstrate how people can live in the light of Jesus Christ day in and day out by doing so ourselves. We must show people how Christian faith effects everything. The reason that it effects everything is that it makes a real difference in life. Inasmuch as some things are *not* effected by the gospel of Jesus Christ, the gospel is ineffective and makes no real difference in life. But the Bible proclaims that everything is effected in one way or another.

Without God's truth people are totally lost, and only the gospel can convert people to God's truth. Congress can make all kinds of laws and pass various resolutions, but until people are converted they will have no genuine interest in changing their ways to serve the glory of God.

Life is good—especially in America. People can sin to their heart's content and still eat three meals a day and still sleep in a warm bed. In this regard it appears that we are nowhere near the end of time. American resources are far from spent. Anticipating this situation Jesus said, "See that you are not troubled, for all these things must occur; but the end is not yet" (Matthew 24:6).

PATIENCE

James counsels patience as we anticipate Christ's return. But he does not mean that we can sit back and do nothing. James likens Christians to farmers, who must plant seeds. We plant God's seed by preaching or presenting the gospel. Then we must wait for God to water it in its season. Christian growth, like all growth, occurs in seasons or cycles, in fits and starts, using the early and later rains.

While we are waiting on God's rain, James further counsels that we establish our hearts. He means that we are to strengthen our understanding of the gospel by studying God's Word. Time is provided during the seasons of growth for study and the establishment of the mind in the teachings of Scripture. We need to use the time wisely because we don't know how much more time we may have. Any of us could not wake up tomorrow.

He further counsels that we should not grumble and groan against one another as we are engaged in establishing our hearts and minds in the teachings of Scripture. None of us are perfect. All of us make mistakes. Rather, we need to encourage and provoke one another to greater effort in God's Word. Using the prophets as an example of steadfast endurance in the Word, we are to press on to our higher calling in Christ. Christians are called to be all that they can be in Christ, and not to settle for anything less than God's best for them.

In spite of what is happening in the world around us, Christians are called to suffer the times—not to merely tolerate them, but to endure them, to bear them without yielding to them, to maintain a steady course amid the storms of life. And the only way to do that is to work to establish ourselves in the faith, to know God's Word so well that nothing can shake us from it.

A storm is coming, and if you are going to weather it, you need to pray to God and keep your powder dry. That is, as Christians we must trust completely on the Lord, for He is the origin and destination of our salvation. But we must also work while it is day, for the night is coming when no one will be able to work (John 9:4).

The death of Jesus Christ on the cross has atoned for all the sins of His people. I hope the you have availed yourselves of Christ's mercy. If you haven't, please waste no time in doing so. But if you already have a personal relationship with Christ, then you must engage the Lord and His Word more seriously.

Are you doing that? My job is to help you do that. I can *help*, but I can't *do* it for you. Rather, we—you and I—need to do it together. That's what Christianity is all about—the fellowship of believers. So, let's believe together.

SANCTIFYING THE TIMES

Paul, a servant of Jesus Christ, a called apostle, separated to the gospel of God (which He had promised beforehand through His prophets in the Holy Scriptures), about His Son, Jesus Christ our Lord, who was made of the seed of David according to the flesh, who was marked out the Son of God in power, according to the Spirit of holiness, by the resurrection from the dead; by whom we have received grace and apostleship, to obedience to the faith among all nations, for His name; among whom you also are the called-out ones of Jesus Christ: to all those who are in Rome, beloved of God, called to be saints. Grace to you and peace from God our Father and the Lord Jesus Christ.

—Romans 1:1-7

We use the word *sanctification* to mean spiritual growth, and it does mean that. But it also has another meaning—set apart. Spiritual growth takes people out of the mainstream where worldly distractions dissipate and attraction to God in Christ integrates. Things that are sanctified are set apart or used exclusively for God's purposes. That's precisely what we mean by spiritual growth.

Christians are set apart to be used by God for His purposes. Our growth in the grace of Christ is one of God's purposes, and that growth can only happen as we are set apart from moral corruption and worldliness.

To grow spiritually is to become more godly and less worldly. It is to be less interested in and motivated by the things of the world and more interested in and motivated by the things of God. Spiritual growth is the process of the separation of godly concerns from worldly concerns in one's own character. It results in an increase in or a deepening of personal moral character qualities. Spiritual growth—sanctification—is not a matter of simply doing godly or church related things, but of actually becoming more godly. It is not a matter of merely performing various duties, but of maturing in the credentials of godliness. The purpose of church membership and involvement is the stimulation of this kind of spiritual growth.

But spiritual growth is not a matter of becoming "spiritual" in some airy-fairy, intellectual, other worldly, withdrawn, introverted or touchy-feely way. Genuine spiritual growth is nothing other than the integration of biblical wisdom in one's actual life through the power and presence of the Holy Spirit by regeneration and discipleship. Spiritual growth is a matter of personal maturity in faithfulness through the integration of Jesus Christ into the practical concerns and aspects of one's life.

In this introduction to Romans Paul said several things about himself that apply to all Christians. He described himself as "separated to the gospel of God" (v. 1). He said that he had "received grace...for obedience to the faith" (v. 5), that all Christians are "the called of Jesus Christ" (v. 6), that church members are "called to be saints" (v. 7). We will deal with these in the reverse order, the order that we experience them. Christians are 1) called, and 2) separated (or sanctified) for 3) obedience to Christ. Our calling separates us, and the purpose of our separation (or sanctification) is gospel obedience.

What has this to do with Christmas? It is the real reason for the season, the very purpose of Christ's incarnation. Christ came in the flesh to call people to gather under His banner. Thus, all Christians are called by God, and those who do not hear God's call to faith in Christ are simply not Christians.

CALL

The Bible speaks of two aspects of Christ's calling people to faith. There is the outward calling by the voice that was done by the lips of Jesus and is now accomplished by the lips of His preachers. As the Verizon television commercial guy says, "Can you hear me now?" Jesus called the disciples, "And immediately...they left their father Zebedee in the boat with the hired servants, and went after Him" (Mark 1:20). The outward call is a physical manifestation—a voice or the printed Word—that is broadcast to all alike. It is God's purpose that every man, woman and child on the face of the earth hear this outward call.

Yet, not everyone will respond with faith to Christ's calling. Many will reject it for a variety of reasons (see Matthew 13:3-9). But those who respond with faith do so because God's calling is efficacious to them. The faithful hear and respond to God's calling because the Lord Himself has prepared them. The Psalmist said that "deep calls to deep" (Psalm 42:7). The depths of God's Holy Spirit calls and touches or effects the depths of the Holy Spirit given by grace to His people. The Spirit calls and the Spirit causes a person to respond.

God's call is a call to selflessness, a call to the mortification of the flesh, or the abandonment of self-concern. It is only by the power of God that anyone can respond because people are by nature selfish and self-concerned. The self will not of itself move toward that which is not in its own self-interest. The self will not willingly abandon itself. Only by truly finding its meaning and purpose in God will people discontinue the meaning and purpose that they find in themselves.

Thus, all Christians, all who abandon self for Christ must be summoned and empowered to do so by a power that is greater than themselves. In a similar way, all Christians—and especially those who serve in a leadership capacity—must be called into service by the Lord. Leaders should not simply respond to the human or organizational need to have a certain number of people in a church or on a committee. Christ doesn't need a hundred people in the church, or six or eight or ten people on a committee to accomplish His purpose. It is not the *quantity* of people that matters to the Lord, but the *quality*. Church leaders must be willing servants of the Lord, able to hear Him and to follow His lead. This is more rare than you might expect.

LEADERS

But who is qualified to serve the Lord? Scripture says that "all have sinned and fall short of the glory of God" (Romans 3:23). If all have sinned, and God cannot tolerate sin, then who is able to fulfill such qualifications? Of themselves, no one! No one is qualified in the flesh to lead God's church. How has the Lord solved this problem? By providing the righteousness of Christ as a robe for His people. Only Christians who are manifestly clothed in the righteousness of Christ are qualified to lead God's church, only those who are consciously and conspicuously born again, blood bought and actually walking in the Spirit.

Does this mean that church leaders are subject to a higher standard? Yes. All Christians are called to manifest godly character qualities, which is a higher standard—and even more is expected of leaders. The examples are so numerous it would be difficult to list them all. Christians are to manifest the fruits of the Spirit—love, joy, peace, patience, kindness, goodness, faithfulness, gentleness, self-control (Galatians 5:22-23). Similarly, all Christians are to abandon godless character qualities—evil thoughts, adulteries, fornications, murders, thefts, covetousness, wickedness, deceit, lewdness, an evil eye, blasphemy, pride, foolishness, etc. (Mark 7:22-23).

Much is expected of Christians, and more is expected of Christian leaders. Like it or not, that's what leadership is about. Does that mean that leaders are subject to the judgment of those they lead? Yes, it does. Scripture itself tells us to evaluate our leaders. Paul said, "Examine yourselves as to whether you are in the faith. Test yourselves. Do you not know yourselves, that Jesus Christ is in you?—unless indeed you are disqualified" (2 Corinthians 13:5). John said, "Beloved, do not believe every spirit, but test the spirits, whether they are of God" (1 John 4:1). The resurrected Christ said, "Because you have kept My command to persevere, I also will keep you from the hour of trial which shall come upon the whole world, to test those who dwell on the earth" (Revelation 3:10).

However, we must realize that we are not to subject others to our own personal judgment. We are in no position to judge anyone else. Therefore, we are not to apply our own standards—what we think is right or wrong, what we like or dislike. Rather, we are to apply God's standards, and we are to apply them first to ourselves. Not only that, but we are to ask others to help us to apply God's standards to ourselves. Then we must be willing to hear what they say about us. And it is out of this spirit of submission to God's standards that leadership qualities are discovered and developed.

Leadership selection should involve the confirmation that a person has received the inward call of the Holy Spirit to serve in such-and-such a capacity. Christian leadership must arise from God's inner calling and experienced as a voluntary response to that call. But that doesn't mean that anyone who wants a leadership position should have it. Rather, the inner call to leadership must be validated (or confirmed, or honored) by those to be led. That's what the process of nomination and election is about. In this way Christian leadership becomes an honorable calling and should be valued by all. Every Christian should aspire to some degree of leadership because leadership should be the normal path for spiritual growth and maturity. But again, we must remember that Christian leadership is servant leadership. Every Christian should aspire to Christian service.

APART

God's calling always produces a separation. Christians are to separate themselves from those who practice ungodliness, those who don't practice Christianity. True faith results in personal moral improvement that leaves behind immorality and ungodliness—slowly perhaps, but truly nonetheless. Godliness and ungodliness cannot coexist. Morality and immorality cannot be mingled very long in the same heart. Godly and ungodly people do not mix because they have radically different interests, desires, and purposes.

Becoming a Christian or growing in Christ often produces a change in the patterns of our lives and our friendships. That is, either our friends find the example of our growing godliness to provide a true motivation for their own change and growth in godliness, or we find ourselves with a different set of friends. The truth is that growth in genuine godliness is not popular. It never has been. It often leads to the loss of friends rather than an increase.

Sinners don't like being around people who are genuine examples of godliness. Those who take godliness seriously are called "wet blankets" because they don't want to do what everybody else does. They are called "boring" because they do not engage in sinful entertainments. They are called "narrow minded" because they are concerned for honesty, justice and moral purity.

The purpose of sanctification or spiritual growth is to increase our obedience to God. The fact that Jesus has taken the burden of the law for His people doesn't mean that He has relieved them from the obligation of obedience to that Law. It just means that obedience is no longer burdensome. It means that punishment for failure to obey perfectly has been taken by Jesus for His people.

In Christ obedience has become a joy because Christ's sacrifice on the cross has removed the fear of failure and punishment. Christians, no longer bound by the Law, *want* to be obedient to the Law—not because they have to, but because such obedience pleases the Lord and is a source of their own personal joy. Then, wanting to obey the Lord in all things, faithful Christians do not need to be bound by the law because they will do everything in their power to obey it. At first a little boy obeys his father in a minimal way because he is afraid of getting a whipping if he doesn't. But as he grows he actively seeks to please his father as much as possible because of the personal satisfaction he receives from pleasing his dad.

Thus obedience to God and His Word is the ultimate end or purpose of spiritual growth. Christians are sanctified by the times in which they live because both the joys and sorrows of the times contribute to their spiritual growth and maturity. Thus, Christians redeem the times by revealing a joy in Christ that outshines the difficulties and trials of the world. Even though we live in evil and difficult times, the glory of obedience to Christ outshines the trials and tribulations of the world.

BEHOLDING THE TIMES

"Behold, the days are coming, declares the LORD, when I will make a new covenant with the house of Israel and the house of Judah, not like the covenant that I made with their fathers on the day when I took them by the hand to bring them out of the land of Egypt, my covenant that they broke, though I was their husband, declares the LORD. But this is the covenant that I will make with the house of Israel after those days, declares the LORD: I will put my law within them, and I will write it on their hearts. And I will be their God, and they shall be my people. And no longer shall each one teach his neighbor and each his brother, saying, 'Know the LORD,' for they shall all know me, from the least of them to the greatest, declares the LORD.' For I will forgive their iniquity, and I will remember their sin no more.'"
—*Jeremiah 31:31-34*

The birth of Jesus in the flesh fulfilled God's ancient plan to redeem mankind from the awful punishment of their sins. God knew long before Adam was tempted in the garden that he would fall. God knew that Adam (humanity) would not be able to resist the temptation of Satan.

So God provided the Law to guide him (humanity) into salvation. God said, "And the Lord God commanded the man, saying, 'Of every tree of the garden you may freely eat; but of the tree of the knowledge of good and evil you shall not eat, for in the day that you eat of it you shall surely die'" (Genesis 2:16-17). Would Adam obey God's Law or would he die in his sins?

He disobeyed, and sin and death have been the lot of humanity ever since. But why did Adam disobey? Why didn't he understand what would happen? The only real way to answer that question without turning it into a speculation jamboree is to ask the question of ourselves. Why do *we* disobey God's commands? Don't we know what will happen? Imagine your five year old daughter coming home from Sunday School having studied the Ten Commandments. She is astute enough to see that you are not in line with one of them —take your choice.

She asks, "Daddy, do you know that cussing is against God's Law?"

"Of course, I know that, darling."

"Then why do you cuss?"

Whatever you say next is the answer we're looking for. The Psalmist put it this way, "Why do the nations rage, And the people plot a vain thing?" (Psalm 2:1). If people know that God is God, why don't they listen to and heed His instructions?

FEAR

What Jeremiah said is that people are afraid of God because they know that He is just, that He will bring sinners to justice for their sins. He must do this because He is just and fair in all things, and He cannot contradict Himself, or act contrary to

His own character. People are afraid of God because they/we are sinners.

It was in the light of this understanding that Jeremiah spoke the words of the Lord in chapter thirty-one. God said that in the future people would know God, not because of His wrath against sinners, but because of His grace and mercy. Jeremiah said that there would be a day when God would forgive their iniquity and not hold their sins against them. In that day God would be known for His forgiveness and mercy.

To know God because of His wrath against sinners is not to know God uniquely or in any special or personal way because God is obligated to relate to all sinners according to His justice and consequent wrath. There is nothing new or unique or personal in this kind of knowledge of God. The whole world knows God by his justice and wrath against sinners. This is the common understanding of God.

But Christians understand that Jeremiah prophesied about the birth of Jesus Christ because in Christ sinners are forgiven. To know God because of His mercy is the unique testimony of Christians. To know the mercy of God is to know God personally because you can't know of God's mercy unless He has shown that mercy to *you* personally. To know God personally is to receive the forgiveness of God. This is the joy of Jesus Christ, the joy of Christmas! By grace a convicted sinner receives pardon. By grace a convicted sinner walks away from death row!

However, in order to fully appreciate the gift of forgiveness, the sinner must realize the seriousness of his sin. Your level of appreciation will be different if you are convicted of jay walking than if you are convicted of murder. A jay walker will be glad that he didn't have to pay the twenty dollar fine, but a convicted murderer will rejoice that his life has been spared.

Most people misunderstand God because they misunderstand the seriousness of their own sin. Until we can fully appreciate the severity of our own sin, we cannot fully appreciate the precious gift of forgiveness. Consequently, God's people never tire of hearing the truth about sin and damnation because it only increases their appreciation for God's gracious mercy.

To further increase our appreciation for God's gracious mercy, Jeremiah said that God would put His Law—His covenant or Word of promise—on the hearts and minds of His people. What was God's covenant or Word of promise? God has said in essence that if people obeyed Him they would be blessed, and if they didn't they would be cursed (Deuteronomy 28). God does not go back on His Word, so that promise is eternal. It will always be true, God will always honor this promise. That was the agreement that God entered into with His people. Notice that it doesn't require anyone's assent. The terms of the covenant (blessings for obedience, curses for disobedience) will be executed upon all people whether or not anyone accepts or believes it. But that was the Old Covenant.

Here in Jeremiah God promised a New Covenant, not different in substance but different in how God would bring about its fulfillment. The New Covenant would be fulfilled in and through Jesus Christ, whereas the Old Covenant could only be kept by strict personal adherence to God's Law. God's eternal covenant required strict obedience. It was a good covenant, worthy of honor and obedience. The only problem was that no one could actually fulfill it. The story of the Old Testament is the story of Israel's failure to be obedient to God. That story came to a head—and to an end—with the destruction of Israel in A.D. 70.

So, was God playing a trick on Israel by requiring something of them that they could not do? Not at all. Rather, the whole purpose of the Old Testament Law was to demonstrate the human inability to satisfy God's demands for righteousness. The purpose was to demonstrate that we human beings cannot do what God requires.

Why would God want to do that? To prepare His people to receive help. If we can do it ourselves, we don't need to be saved. We just need to be properly encouraged to do the right thing. But if we can't do it ourselves, then we will need help. Someone will have to do it for us, or give us the power and ability to do it. Our inability shows us our need for God.

Have you ever tried to help someone who didn't want help? People are independent and enjoy being independent. People would rather do it themselves. Surely you know this. You can't help people until they admit or realize that they need help. It's a natural human characteristic. So, God was simply demonstrating to all humanity that we are unable to save ourselves, that we must rely on God to provide salvation.

Jesus Christ is the help that God provides. Unfortunately, most people will not avail themselves of Christ's help until they have discovered that they can't do it themselves. This is the problem that God addressed when He said that He would put His Law on people's hearts and in their minds.

What does it mean to have something "on your heart?" The Hebrew word is *qereb*, which indicates the seat or source of thought and emotion. When something is on your heart, you genuinely desire it, you crave it, you don't ever forget it. When you were courting your spouse, he or she was on your heart. Lovers tend to think of each other all the time. They don't forget each other. Jeremiah alluded to the marriage covenant because God's covenant is a kind of marriage covenant.

What was it that God was going to put on the hearts of His people? His Law. The broadest understanding of God's Law is His Word, or the Bible. God would cause His people to want to study and know and live in obedience to Scripture. When Scripture is on your heart, you can't wait to read it again, to discover every nuance about it. Just as separated lovers pine for each other, God's people yearn for Scripture.

That yearning then brings us to the next element of God's promise given through Jeremiah. God said that He would put Scripture in the minds of His people. That is, they would know God's Word. No one would need to teach them because they would already love it and read it and study it and memorize it. They would live for it, think and ruminate on it throughout the day and into the night. Like lovers, they would be possessed by God's Word. That's what Jeremiah was talking about.

You there yet?

Understanding The Times

The scepter shall not depart from Judah, nor the ruler's staff from between his feet, until tribute comes to him; and to him shall be the obedience of the peoples. Binding his foal to the vine and his donkey's colt to the choice vine, he has washed his garments in wine and his vesture in the blood of grapes. His eyes are darker than wine, and his teeth whiter than milk.   —*Genesis 49:10-12*

In order to understand the times in which we live, we must possess some understanding of the broad sweep of salvation history. Without the knowledge of God's purpose in history, the various events that so engulf our attention will be perceived as a kind of random deterioration of society rather than the intentional unfolding of God's purpose. To see the broad sweep of God's hand through history we turn to Genesis.

We could have turned to Genesis 3:15, the first biblical allusion to the coming of Christ, "I will put enmity Between you and the woman, And between your seed and her Seed; He shall bruise your head, And you shall bruise His heel." Here is described the great struggle between the sons of men and the sons of God, between people guided by their own resources and people guided by the Word of God. This is the classic struggle that unfolds throughout the pages of the Bible. These two forces will remain mutually antagonistic until we see the New Jerusalem coming down from heaven as prophesied in Revelation at the end of history.

For our purposes today we turn to the Shiloh prophecy (Genesis 49:10). The Hebrew word *Shiyloh* is of uncertain origin. Roughly translated it means "he whose it is, that which belongs to him, tranquility." *Shiloh* describes the inner experience of peace and serenity that comes over a land or a people or a family when the owner or the highest authority comes to claim His rightful ownership.

In this regard Shiloh is not merely a prophecy of the coming of Christ, but is a prophecy of the final acceptance of Christ's authority. Therefore, it is a prophecy of the end of the great struggle between the sons of men and the sons of God. This struggle is depicted in Scripture as the struggle between those who reject God and those who follow God. We see the struggle, for instance, between Cain and Able, between Enoch and Enosh, between Jacob and Esau, between Noah and the sinful world of his day, in the civil war between Israel and Judah, between the prophets and the people of Israel, between Jesus and the Pharisees, and between Paul and the Judiasers.

CONFLICT

It is quite possible that you are not aware of this basic biblical conflict because it has not been taught in the popular literature for several decades. However, it belongs to the Christian church by right of inheritance. It is part of the deposit of Christian history that has been handed down through the generations. Unfortunately, many contemporary Christians have a curious distaste for the historic treasures of the church.

The lack of the popularity of Christian history and doctrine has resulted in a debilitating amnesia among Christians in our day.

Yet, we must understand that even this amnesia is not unique to our age, but has plagued God's people for eons. God's people are forever forgetting, ignoring, or otherwise belittling the chief articles of the faith for a mess of potage of one sort or another. As Esau sold his birthright for the temporary satisfaction of his belly, so many throughout history have turned from the central teachings of the Lord to the excitements and successes of their own concerns and imaginations. This plague resurfaces every three or four generations in Scripture, and has continued that general pattern throughout history. It has returned in our time with a vengeance.

The pattern works generally as follows: a generation of people have a direct experience of God, i.e., the crossing of the Red Sea, or fire come down from heaven, or a revival breaks out. Those who witness it first hand are converted beyond the shadow of a doubt. They then teach their children about the Lord and His mighty works. These children, then, learn about God second hand from their parents. Their faith is not as marked or as strong as that of their parents. When they then have children they in turn are not as conscientious about teaching their children about the faith because it had been only second hand information to them. These third generation children then only hear occasional odd stories about their grandparents' faith and experience. But when these third generation children have children of their own, and the grandparents who had known God personally are dead, there is little impetus to teach about God or Jesus Christ, there is little real knowledge of the Lord to be passed on. You can't teach what you don't know. Those children, then, grow up without knowing the Lord, without experience, exposure or teaching.

FORGOTTEN

The Lord and His ways are often forgotten every third or fourth generation, until someone personally rediscovers them and is converted and calls God's people to revival. Thus the need for revival among God's people is actually a black mark on the progressive purposes of the Lord's salvation history. To say that we are in need of revival is to say that we have forgotten the things of God. Said another way, revival is needed because the concerns of men have eclipsed the concerns of God. That's where we are in history today. We live in the midst of great darkness and confusion concerning the primary articles of the faith. The churches are in need of revival because they have grown cold and/or because they are confused and/or unconcerned about God's truth.

Our mission, then, the mission of the church in our day is a mission of recovery. Because God does not change, and because God's basic plan of salvation does not and has not changed throughout history, we see the weakness and ineffectiveness of the churches and must confess that we (contemporary Christians) have again departed from God, from a right understanding, a right teaching of the chief articles of the faith.

We know that God has not left us. God does not and will not leave His people. The fault is ours. The church errs when she departs from her historical teachings and practices, from her first love. The original passions and practices of Christianity are woven into the fabric of history. The study of Christian history does not detract from or draw us away from our "first love" (Revelation 2:4). Rather, it establishes it.

The Old Testament Prophets accused the Priests of their day of such departure. Jesus accused the Pharisees of such departure. Paul accused the Judiasers of such departure. The Reformers of the 16th Century accused Rome and her priests of such departure. It is neither new or unusual that the chief articles of the faith get obscured. It is a recurring theme in biblical and Christian history.

Therefore, in order to be faithful, in order to keep from or to recover from such departures, we must understand and honor the historical, evangelical teachings and practices of the church. To do less than this is to be part of the problem rather than part of the solution. Because God does not change, His Word does not change. His promises do not change. His methods of salvation do not change. God and his Word are unique because they do not change. They are the one constant throughout history by which the church is guided.

But everything else changes—people, places, dates, issues, and especially the ancient Greek god—technology. Everything changes except God and His Word. God is the North Star around which everything else moves. Everything that God does contributes to His self-revelation in Jesus Christ. The Old Testament Prophets pointed forward to God's full revelation in Christ, the New Testament Apostles pointed back to God's full revelation in Christ. The purpose of God's church in history is always and forever to point to God's full revelation in Jesus Christ.

Jacob's prophecy regarding Judah and the coming of Shiloh indicates that God had intended to send Jesus as the Messiah of the whole world from the very beginning of time. Here is prophesied the lineage of Jesus through the line of Judah. Of course the prophecy pointed to David's kingship as well. King David played a key role in the Messianic prophecy. But reading the history of David's kingship we see that the Shiloh prophecy was not fulfilled by David. Peace and serenity do not describe David's reign, nor Solomon's. Rather, the

Shiloh prophecy pointed through the founding of David's kingdom to the coming of Christ.

RETURN

Yet, in every respect it cannot be said that peace and serenity describe the advent of Christ either. Rather, history since Christ has been every bit as barbarous as history before Him. Yet, because we know that the Shiloh prophecy points beyond David to Christ, we also know that it points to the completion of God's promise in the establishment of Christ's kingdom—His second coming. In Bethlehem He came in mercy for the forgiveness of sin. In the future He will come on the clouds in glory for the establishment of His justice. Lord, have mercy!

In the Shiloh prophecy we see that the septre, the symbol of authority, belonged Judah and would be fully established in Christ because of "the obedience of the people" (v. 10). When the Owner came, what belonged to Him would be bound to "the vine." Jesus identified Himself as the vine (John 15:5). Thus, what belongs to God will be bound to Christ. But notice that the donkey's colt—the offspring—is also bound. Not only are the people of God bound to Christ in obedience, but their children are also bound. This is a repetition of the promise given to Abraham, "In your seed all the nations of the earth shall be blessed, because you have obeyed My voice" (Genesis 22:18).

We know that in Christ we are not saved because of our obedience, rather, we cannot even be obedient without the power of Christ's Holy Spirit to change our hearts and minds. The allusion Jacob made was that the clothes of those bound to the vine would be washed in the blood of grapes, or the blood of the Lamb since the Lamb and the Vine are one. Thus the

Shiloh prophecy is a prophecy of salvation by the grace of Christ's sacrifice. Salvation would belong to those wrapped in the blood-dyed cloak of Christ's righteousness. The peace and serenity provided by obedience to God's Word could belong to no others, only to those who have been blood bought, who have been regenerated by the power and presence of the Holy Spirit.

For this purpose God sent Jesus Christ His only begotten Son, our Lord; Who was conceived by the Holy Spirit, born of the Virgin Mary, suffered under Pontius Pilate, was crucified, dead, and buried; who descended into hell; on the third day He rose again from the dead; and ascended into heaven. The same Jesus Christ sits at the right hand of God, the Father Almighty; from thence shall He come to judge the quick an the dead. For this purpose God sent the Holy Spirit to establish the one holy universal Christian church, the communion of saints, the forgiveness of sins, the resurrection of the body, and the life everlasting.

It's all true, and it continues to unfold in our presence, in our time, even here. Praise be to God in Jesus Christ!

WHAT IN THE WORLD IS ROSS DOING?

In 1983 I had an experience that culminated in 1985 in what is called regeneration. Ordained at First Congregational Church, Berkeley, California (1981), after earning a Master of Divinity degree at Pacific School of Religion (1980), I was confronted by the reality of the Bible as I taught the Bethel Series Bible Study Program at a church I was serving in St. Louis, Missouri. I had read and studied the Bible for many years, but the Bethel Series opened it up to me in a new way. It became real, and it changed me.

I began preaching differently from that time forward, as if the Bible was real history about real people. My preaching disturbed some of the people in various liberal churches that I served. Others in those same churches came to life, much as I had. I decided to preserve my preaching for later reflection and evaluation. That effort turned into a two-volume book, *The Work at Zion—A Reckoning*, 2 vols. (1996), which provides a kind of record of my changing theological perspective.

At the same time, the simple-minded, pie-in-the-sky, other-worldly, wishful-thinking of some of my new conservative friends disturbed me. It seemed to me that people from both ends of the political spectrum had misunderstood the Bible, albeit in different ways. So, I set out to see if the kind of

43

biblical misunderstanding that I observed among various people I knew was new. Were the contemporary churches involved in something new? I discovered that they were not. There is a long history of misunderstanding the Bible.

I turned to the book of James which provided a corrective to the early church. Already in the First Century the church had veered from the truth of the gospel. James saw it and spoke to it. I brought James' corrective to light in *Practically Christian —Applying James Today* (2006).

Looking for the original source of the problem of biblical misunderstanding, I began studying the story of Jesus' ministry. If the doctrines of grace were true, then Jesus would have preached them. He did. And sure enough, almost everyone had misunderstood Jesus during his earthly ministry. So I detailed this story about Jesus and His friends in *Marking God's Word—Understanding Jesus* (2006.

Seeking some practical advice about the right way to live as a Christian, I then turned to a study of the Book of Proverbs for some practical advice. The difficulty for many Christians is that Proverbs predates the ministry of Jesus. But it does not predate the reality of Christ. Historic theology teaches that the Christian faith is founded on the eternal consistency of God. God does not change, nor does God's wisdom. So I began looking for Christ in Proverbs and found Him on every page. That study became *The Wisdom of Jesus Christ in the Book of Proverbs* (2006).

I then picked up the continuing story of the gospel in the Book of Acts, only to find that people misunderstood Paul in the same ways that they had misunderstood Jesus—until the dispensation of the Holy Spirit. Paul took up the gospel of Jesus Christ, teaching and preaching as Jesus did, and all hell was rallied against him. That story is found in *Acts of Faith—Kingdom Advancement* (2007).

Arsy Varsy—Reclaiming the Gospel in First Corinthians (2008) was begun at Covenant PCA in Vienna, WV (now defunct), in order to provide a deeper understanding of the American church situation and its current similarity with the ancient church at Corinth, and the reality of contemporary backwardness. Covenant was a PCA new church start, and was struggling with how to be a successful church. Paul spoke to these same concerns in the large, influential and successful church at Corinth.

Varsy Arsy—Proclaiming the Gospel in Second Corinthians (2009) followed as Covenant PCA in Vienna, WV, dissolved and/or morphed into the Mid-Ohio Valley Reformed Fellowship (also defunct). The issues that Paul spoke to in Second Corinthians have proven to be as applicable as those in First Corinthians. Many of the Corinthians had difficulty understanding Paul. Will we never learn?!

In 2009 I decided to revisit an earlier, unfinished work then titled, *Nothing But Christ—Another Look at Colossians*. This book had been a test case for Wipf & Stock to sample the quality of their publishing. The manuscript needed to be finished, so I completed it in 2009 it and published it in 2010 under the title: *Colossians—Christos Singularis* (2010).

Thinking that people might appreciate a practical guide to Christian living, I decided to work through Jesus' Sermon on the Mount, which resulted in *Rock Mountain Creed—Jesus' Sermon on the Mount* (2011).

Once Pilgrim Platform Books was up and running, I decided to resurrect some of my sermon series from Putnam Congregational Church in Marietta. *It's About Time* (2008),

Engagement (2008), and *The Big Ten* (2008) are sermon series preached in the late 1990s, but dusted off and reworked for a broader audience.

Along the way I discovered John Williamson Nevin, and in my enthusiasm to understand him I reworked and republished his 1846 book, *The Mystical Presence–A Vindication of the Reformed and Calvinistic Doctrine of the Holy Eucharist,* as *The True Mystery of the Mystical Presence* (2011).

In my research of the history of Marietta, Ohio (*The Religious History of Marietta in the Nineteenth Century* (1903, 2012), I discovered the first recipient of an honorary degree by Marietta College: Edward Beecher, son of Lyman Beecher and brother of Harriet Beecher Stowe. I was so enthralled by his treatment of Christian history, and his maltreatment by his peers, that I republished his main works from the mid-1800s: *Conflict Of Ages–The Great Debate of the Moral Relations of God and Man* (1853, 2012) and *Concord of Ages–The Individual And Organic Harmony Of God And Man* (1860, 2013).

In response to a friend who had a question about the end times references in the book of 2nd Peter, came *Peter's Vision of Christ's Purpose in First Peter* (2011) and *Peter's Vision of The End in Second Peter* (2012).

I have written poetry since my adolescence. My mother was a poet. And I have continued to write sporadically. The appreciation of poetry lies in the eye of the reader. So if you have an eye for poetry, you might look at my collection: *Poet Tree—Root, Branch, and Sap* (2013). But definitely check out my mother's poetry: *Inside Out woman—Collected Poetry, Doris M. Ross* (2014).

For years I have been frustrated with smart people who dismiss Jesus, many who embrace the modern idea of sustainability. It occurred to me that the goal of the sustainability concern is a lot like what the Bible calls eternal life. So, I worked through Ephesians with this in mind: *Ephesians— Recovering the Vision of a Sustainable Church in Christ* (2013).

About this same time I read through the Chronological Bible, which I highly recommend. It helps us see the big story of the Bible and to keep from getting lost in the details. That then led to a re-reading of Galatians from Paul's perspective, which provided, for me, a new understanding of Paul. I titled it *Galatians—Backstory/Christstory* (2015).

John Saggio, whom I have never met, sent me an unsolicited copy of his gargantuan, self-published book, *The Destiny of Israel and the Twilight of Christianity*, subtitled: "In Quest of the Meaning and Significance of the Hebrew and Greek Scriptures." Saggio taught philosophy at Mesa Community College.

Saggio's book is a thorough defense of Preterism, making the case from both the Old and New Testaments that all biblical prophecy has been completely fulfilled. I agree with Saggio's conclusion that the advent of Christ fulfilled the Old Testament, but I take exception with his idea that the destruction of the Temple and Jerusalem in A.D. 70 completely fulfilled the New Testament. So I answered his argument with *God's Great Plan for the Whole World* (2019).

A decade or more ago I preached a series on the miracles of Jesus in John's gospel. The idea was that John, who wrote much later than Matthew, Mark, and Luke, provided a correction or a different perspective on Jesus' miracles. I knew that it would be challenging for many people, but I decided to publish it: *John's Miracles—Seeing Beyond Our Expectations* (2019).

I've had a ministry website for a very long time, and have written many articles about the church and the contemporary culture. I knew that people would not take the time and effort to read my blog online, so I decided to make it easier by publishing the articles in a single volume: *Essays on Church— Ordinary Christianity for the World* (2020).

A friend asked me about the idea of the rapture found in First and Second Thessalonians. So I addressed his concern in *Thessalonians—Thorn, Thistle, and Throne* (2021).

When I became the pastor of St. Paul's Evangelical Church, Marietta, Ohio (2022), I began reading up on the history of the church, which involves Mercersberg Seminary in Pennsylvania, where John Williamson Nevin was the President. I discovered another professor: Emmanuel V. Gerhart, who wrote *The Institutes of the Christian Religion* (1891, 1894). I decided to update an annotate them in several smaller volumes: *Institutes Of The Christian Religion*, Vols. 1&2, Vol. 3 (2023, to be continued, God willing).

As the 45th pastor of St. Paul's I thought it was time to write a history of the church. However, I could not find much information on most of the previous pastors. So I tied the history to the major church events of her history, which involved several denominations and their histories. The result is *The Heritage of St. Paul's Evangelical Church* (2024).

As companion volumes I have included my sermons at St. Paul's in three volumes (so far). Not knowing where to begin preaching at St. Paul's I turned to the Lectionary, which I had not done for a long time: *GoodNews—Evangel 2022, Good-News Evangel 2023, GoodNews—Evangel 2024*, and *GoodNews —Reformation Reloaded* (2026).

I have labored to teach people how to read Scripture with the eyes of faith, to see the richness and depth of the biblical perspective. And it often involves disabusing people of some wrong (unbiblical) assumptions and expectations about the Bible, about ministry, about the church, about the world, etc. I'm convinced that those wrong assumptions and expectations are the very things that have gutted the churches, bled into the larger society, and continue wreaking havoc. Thus, the condition of the Christian church is at the center of our the world's current and eternal problems.

The solution is not to bring more lost people into the pews. As needed as that is, it won't help until the churches get faithfulness right. People are to be saved into the churches, but the culture of the churches is no different than the culture of the world. Few churches have any idea of what a biblically faithful Christian life would look like. Most churches just slap Bible study and prayer onto their existing worldly lifestyles and call it Christian. Consequently, the need of the hour is not evangelism, but sanctification—growth and maturity in the faith.

I call my approach to the Bible presuppositional Trinitarianism, by which I mean that I simply assume the doctrine of the Trinity to be true. In addition, the image in which humanity has been created is a reflection of God. And the most unique thing about God is His Trinitarianism. This means that humanity has been crated in the image of God's Trinity: Father, Son, and Holy Spirit. We are like God in this regard, but are a distant, dark, reflection of God's Trinity. There is not a one-to-one correspondence, so we can think of it as being composed of mind, body, and spirit; or in a corporate sense as individual, group, and the wholeness of humanity. This provides a biblical analysis that is deep, granular, at times philosophical, but also surprisingly simple. Is it true? Is it valuable? I think so, but self evaluation is never a trustworthy guide. Time with tell, God willing.

Phillip A. Ross

Marietta, Ohio

2025